I Can Write Reports

Anita Ganeri

Raintree

www.raintreepublishers.co.uk
Visit our website to find out more information about Raintree books.

To order:
☎ Phone 0845 6044371
📄 Fax +44 (0) 1865 312263
📧 Email myorders@raintreepublishers.co.uk

Customers from outside the UK please telephone +44 1865 312262

Raintree is an imprint of Capstone Global Library Limited, a company incorporated in England and Wales having its registered office at 7 Pilgrim Street, London, EC4V 6LB – Registered company number: 6695582

Text © Capstone Global Library Limited 2013
First published in hardback in 2013
First published in paperback in 2013
The moral rights of the proprietor have been asserted.

Edited by Daniel Nunn, Rebecca Rissman, and Sian Smith
Designed by Victoria Allen
Picture research by Elizabeth Alexander
Original illustrations © Capstone Global Library Ltd 2013
Illustrated by Victoria Allen and Darren Lingard
Production by Victoria Fitzgerald
Originated by Capstone Global Library Ltd
Printed and bound in China by Leo Paper Products Ltd

ISBN 978 1 406 23834 1 (hardback)
16 15 14 13 12
10 9 8 7 6 5 4 3 2 1

ISBN 978 1 406 23841 9 (paperback)
17 16 15 14 13
10 9 8 7 6 5 4 3 2 1

British Library Cataloguing in Publication Data
Ganeri, Anita, 1961-
   Reports. -- (I can write)
   1. Report writing--Juvenile literature.
   I. Title II. Series
   808'.02-dc23

Acknowledgements
We would like to thank the following for permission to reproduce photographs and artworks: Alamy p.6 (© purewhite life); iStockphoto p.24 (© Nina Shannon); Rex Features p.27 (Lili Forberg); Shutterstock pp.8 (© bikeriderlondon), 9 (© AISPIX), 13 (© Talvi), 13, 17 (© vector-RGB), 14 (© Lightspring), 14 (© Seleznev Oleg), 15 (© Pichugin Dmitry), 16 (© Vaclav Volrab), 17 , 17 (© Ra Juergen Kraft), 18 © jossnat), (19 © megainarmy), 19 (© ysfylmz 19 (© kots), 20 (© Lorelyn Medina), 20 (© Oleksiy Mark), 21 (© charles taylor), 22 (© alexall), 23 (© mathom), 25 (© Marjannek de Jong); Superstock p.4 (© Image Source), 5 (© Blend Images 7 (© Corbis), 10 (© Blend Images), 11 (© Fancy Collection).

Every effort has been made to contact copyright holders of material reproduced in this book. Any omissions will be rectified in subsequent printings if notice is given to the publisher.

Contents

Some words are shown in bold, **like this**. You can find out what they mean in the glossary on page 30.

What is writing?

Writing is when you put words down on paper or type them onto a computer screen. Writing clearly helps your readers to understand what you mean.

What do you like writing about?

Write a report about something that interests you.

There are many different types of writing. This book is about reports. Reports are a type of **non-fiction**. This means that they are about facts.

What is a report?

A report is a piece of writing that gives the reader facts and information about a subject. The writer describes what things are, or were, like.

This report tells you about a bird in a zoo.

Plan your report before you start writing.

In a report, you do not have to write the events in the order that they happened. You can write them in any order, but you still need to plan your report carefully.

Lots of reports

There are lots of different kinds of reports. You can read reports in magazines and newspapers. Book reviews and school projects are also reports.

What sort of reports do you like reading?

A guidebook has reports about interesting places to visit.

Reports give information and help readers to find out more. Information leaflets, tourist guidebooks, and online **encyclopedias** are also reports.

Fact finding

A report is about facts, so you need to find out all about your topic. This is called doing research. You can find facts in books, newspapers and magazines, on TV, or on the internet.

Research your topic before you start writing.

Think about where your information has come from. Not everything you read will be correct.

Keep a notebook and pen with you. Jot down any interesting facts you find. Keep a list of where your facts came from. Try to make sure they come from places you can trust.

Getting ideas

It can be difficult to work out what to write. These tips may help you. Try noting down everything you know about your topic. This is called **mind mapping**.

This is a mind map for the topic 'elephants'.

ELEPHANTS

huge animals

grey skin

tusks

long trunks

eat plants

live in Africa and India

You could also try drawing a diagram called a spidergram. Write your topic in a circle. Then write lots of connected words or ideas around the outside.

The word 'elephants' is the spider's body. The words around it are the spider's legs.

huge animals

grey skin

eat plants

ELEPHANTS

tusks

live in Africa and India

long trunks

Planning a report

Before you start writing, you need to plan your report. Start by thinking of a title. It should be quite short, but needs to tell your reader what your report is about.

Keep your title short and simple.

All about deserts

By [name]

Next, organize your information. Divide your report into sections. The first section introduces the topic that you are writing about. The last section sums things up.

Deserts are very hot and dry. They are sandy or rocky.

The first few **sentences** tell the reader what your report is about.

Writing style

Your writing style means the way you write. In a report, your writing style should be quite **formal** because you do not know the people you are writing for.

Snails don't move very fast. ✗

Snails do not move very fast. ✓

It is better to use 'do not' than 'don't' in formal writing.

Break your writing up into **paragraphs**. This will make it easier to read. A paragraph is a group of **sentences** about the same thing.

This paragraph has four sentences.

Dinosaurs ate lots of food. Some dinosaurs only ate plants. Some only ate meat. Some ate plants and meat.

Useful words

Write your report in the **present tense** if you are describing how things are. You can use the **past tense** if you are writing about something that has already happened.

The racing cars are going very fast around the track.

'Are going' is the present tense of the verb 'to go'.

The racing cars went very fast around the track.

'Went' is the past tense of the verb 'to go'.

Use words that help to describe your topic and tell your reader more about it. Here are some useful words if you are writing a report about racing cars.

Can you think of any more useful words about racing cars?

<u>Useful words</u>

track

racing driver

fast

laps

chequered flag

pit stop

Book review

A book review is a report about a book that you have read. Start by writing down the title and author of the book. Then describe what the book is about.

Top Ten Toys

By John Cooper

This book looks at lots of toys. It tells you which toys children like best.

Start by saying what the book is about.

Next, you might write down what you think about the book. Do you like it? Is it interesting? Is it clearly written? Does it make you want to find out more about the topic?

<u>Useful words</u>

funny

interesting

well organized

easy to read

eye-catching

You can write reviews of books, films, or music.

Newspaper report

A newspaper report tells you about
a piece of news that has happened.
Start your report with a catchy **headline**
and first line. This will help to grab
your reader's interest.

<u>**Dino dig delight!**</u>

**Scientists dug up the fossil
bones of the biggest dinosaur
that had ever lived.**

By [your name]

Remember to
put your name
on your report.

Next, describe what happened, and when and where it happened. You can add **quotes** from people who were there at the time and saw what happened.

A quote is the exact words that a person has said.

"I've never seen anything so big in my life!" said a scientist.

Balanced report

A **balanced** report is a report about an **issue** that gives both sides of an argument. It presents lots of different facts and ideas. Then the reader can make his or her own mind up about the issue.

SCHOOL UNIFORM
Is it a good idea?

Try writing a balanced report about wearing a school uniform.

Write down reasons why wearing a school uniform is a good idea or a bad idea. Talk to pupils and teachers at your school to find out what they think.

Use **bullet points** for each new point.

SCHOOL UNIFORM
Is it a good idea?

Yes!
- You do not need to think what to wear every day.
- It looks smart.
- It shows which school you go to.

No!
- It makes everyone look the same.
- It looks boring.
- It is old-fashioned.

Write a report

Try writing a report about a famous person. It could be someone such as your favourite pop star. Think of a list of questions. Then try to research the answers.

Where were they born?

How did they start singing?

What music do they like?

What's their favourite colour?

What other questions could you ask?

Use pictures to go with the information you find out. You can use artworks or photographs. Pictures help to show readers what you are writing about.

Each picture needs a **caption**. This explains what the picture shows.

This is a picture of the singers.

Top tips for writing reports

1. Read lots of different reports. The more you read, the better your own writing will become.

2. Read your report through when you have finished. Check your facts and spelling. Correct anything that is wrong.

3. If you find good books or websites for your research, keep a note of them. You might need them later.

4. Double-check any information you find on the internet. You need to make sure that your facts are correct.

5. Use pictures, photos, charts, and diagrams to explain your information.

6. Give each section or **paragraph** a heading. This helps to divide up the text and makes it easier to read.

7. If you get stuck for ideas, try writing down whatever comes into your head about a topic. This is called automatic writing.

8. Keep practising! Writing is just like drawing or painting. You need to keep practising.

Glossary

balanced to give both sides of an argument

bullet points small circles that are used instead of numbers in a list

caption words that describe a picture or photograph

encyclopedia book made up of reports about many different topics

formal language that is correct and follows the rules

headline title of a newspaper report

issue important topic

mind mapping thinking of everything you can about a subject

non-fiction writing that is about real people or things

paragraph group of sentences

past tense form of a verb that describes something that happened in the past

present tense form of a verb that describes something that is happening now

quote writing the exact words that a person has said

sentence group of words that makes sense on its own

Find out more

Books

Getting to Grips with Grammar series, Anita Ganeri
(Raintree Publishing, 2012)

How to Write Reports, Anne Faundez
(QED Publishing, 2008)

Websites

www.bbc.co.uk/schools/ks1bitesize/literacy

www.bbc.co.uk/schools/ks2bitesize/english/writing

Index